What's it like to be a...

TRUCK DRIVER

Written by Judith Stamper
Illustrated by George Ulrich

Troll Associates

Special Consultants: Joseph Carretta and Michael Parkes
of Carretta Trucking, Inc., Paramus, New Jersey.

Library of Congress Cataloging-in-Publication Data

Stamper, Judith Bauer.
   Truck driver / by Judith Stamper; illustrated by George Ulrich.
     p.   cm.—(What's it like to be a...)
   Summary: Describes different kinds of trucks, their variations in
design and function, and the duties and activities of their drivers.
   ISBN 0-8167-1424-X (lib. bdg.)   ISBN 0-8167-1425-8 (pbk.)
   1. Truck driving—Juvenile literature. [1. Trucks. 2. Truck
driving. 3. Occupations.] I. Ulrich, George, ill. II. Title.
III. Series.
TL230.3.S73 1989
629.28'44'023—dc19   88-10039

What's it like to be a...
TRUCK DRIVER

Tank Truck

Semitrailer
Truck

M&M

FRED'S FAST FREIGHT

GAS

Refrigerated Van

Semitrailer

Tractor

Dump Truck

Zoom! Cars and trucks rush along a busy highway. Alongside the highway sits a small truck stop. All kinds of trucks are parked there.

Inside, truck drivers eat good food. They tell each other stories. They laugh and relax. This is their time to rest from their long hours on the road.

Outside, many drivers are busy getting fuel for their trucks. Some trucks use gasoline. Many big trucks use diesel fuel.

The fuel is pumped into huge tanks on the trucks. These big trucks use a lot of fuel!

Air Horn

Rearview Mirror

Running Lights

Exhaust Stack

Air Vent

Hand Hold

ACE

Radiator

DIESEL

Fuel Tank

Hub

Headlights

Bumper

Fuel Pump

Fuel Line

7

Air Shield

Air Filter

Mud Flap

Step

Soon, the drivers are ready to get on the road again. They wave good-bye to their friends. Their trucks are full of cargo. Groceries, lumber, toys, and books—all are on their way to stores and warehouses. Trucks carry goods all across the country.

Cab

*10-Wheel
Concrete Mixer*

18-Wheel Tanker Rig

Dump Truck

Cab Over Tractor

Flat-Bed
Log-Hauler Rig

Sleeper Cab

Refrigerated Van

STATE MOVERS

Cab Over Sleeper

18-Wheel Box Rig

Truck drivers transport cargo of all shapes
and sizes. Their trucks are as different as what
they carry.

Tank

Tank trucks are built to carry liquid cargo. This tank-truck driver is transporting milk. Today she will deliver the milk to a dairy plant. There the milk will be put into containers. By morning, the milk will be in the store, ready to buy.

Fill Hatch

Exhaust Stack

FARM

Discharge Valves

Step

Directional Signal

Bumper

Radiator

Headlights

Fuel Tank

Tankers also carry orange juice, paint, chemicals, and many other liquids. Tank trucks are easy to fill and empty. The liquid is pumped in and out through a hose or pipe.

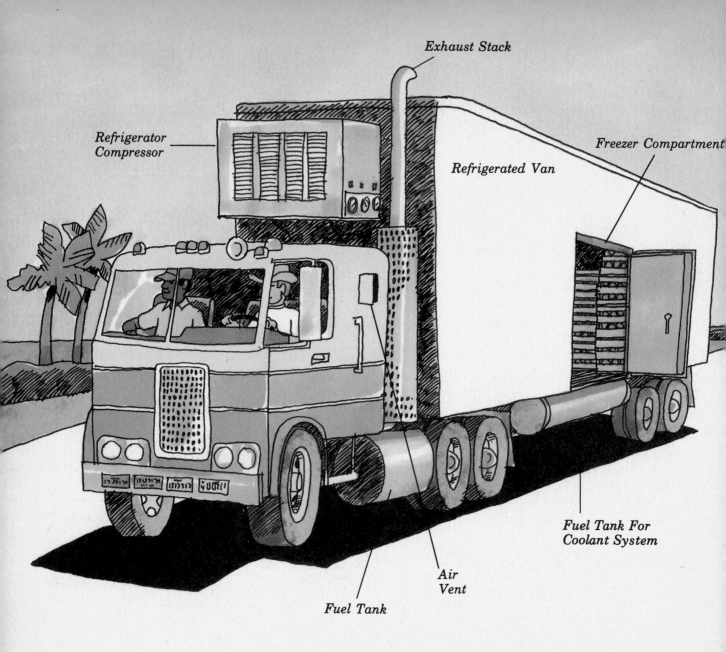

Exhaust Stack

Refrigerator Compressor

Refrigerated Van

Freezer Compartment

Fuel Tank For Coolant System

Air Vent

Fuel Tank

This special truck has a refrigerated van. It carries cargo that must stay at a certain temperature. This driver is carrying fruit from Florida. Delicious oranges and juicy lemons are on their way to market.

14

Another kind of refrigerated van carries meat. The meat is hung on rails from the roof of the truck. This driver is delivering beef to a supermarket.

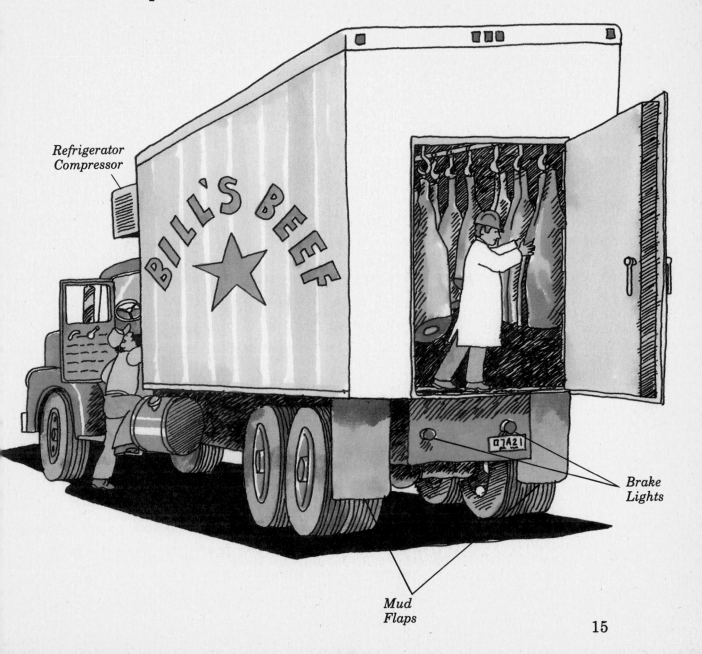

Refrigerator Compressor

Brake Lights

Mud Flaps

A livestock van carries live animals. This kind of truck has holes on its sides. The holes give the animals air to breathe.

Small animals travel in vans with different levels or decks. The decks make it possible to carry more animals at once.

Livestock Van

Mail Truck

Diesel Locomotive

17

Exhaust Stack

Cab

Boom Lines

Boom

Crawler Tracks

A flat-bed trailer transports large cargo. The bed, or bottom, of the trailer is long, flat, and open. The truck's engine is powerful—it has to be to carry heavy loads.

18

Block

Hook

Flat-Bed Trailer

Cranes load lumber, steel, and other heavy materials on the trailer. The cargo is tied down with ropes or steel cables. This driver is delivering building materials to a construction site.

The biggest trucks are tractor trailers. They have two main parts. The front is the tractor part. It is the cab and engine. The back is the trailer. It carries the cargo.

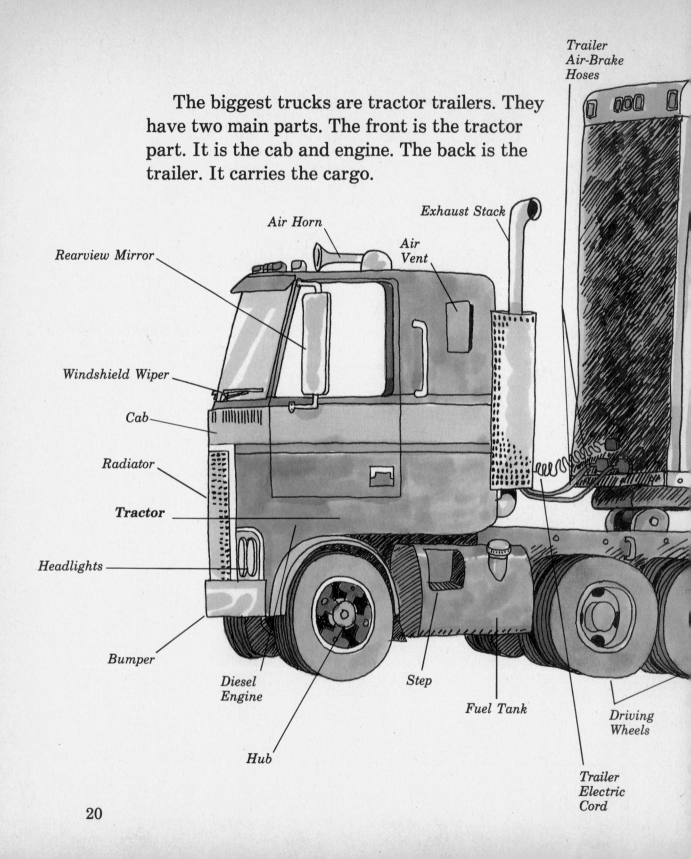

Trailer Air-Brake Hoses

Air Horn

Exhaust Stack

Air Vent

Rearview Mirror

Windshield Wiper

Cab

Radiator

Tractor

Headlights

Bumper

Diesel Engine

Hub

Step

Fuel Tank

Driving Wheels

Trailer Electric Cord

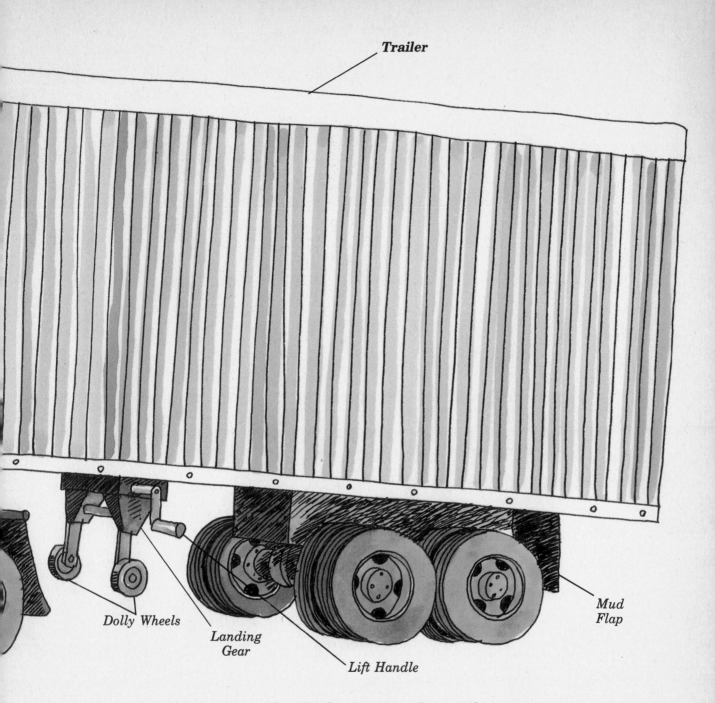

Trailer

Dolly Wheels

Landing Gear

Lift Handle

Mud Flap

The bigger a load, the bigger the trailer must be. The bigger a trailer, the more wheels it needs.

Speedometer

Steering Wheel

The driver of a tractor trailer must be skilled and strong. Driving such a big truck is not easy, and there are many gauges and controls to watch. This driver has been specially trained to handle a tractor trailer. His truck is carrying paper to be used for printing newspapers.

Instrument Gauges

Gearshift
Lever

Differential
Shift

CB Radio

CB Microphone

10301

171702

Smoke Stack

Lifeboat

Gangway

Fork Lift

Flat-Bed
Trailer

Container trucks have bodies that can be lifted off their beds. That way, the containers can easily be moved from trucks to ships, or to train cars, or even to huge airplanes.

24

Gantry Crane

Mast

Boom

Container Ship

Bollard

Container

The goods inside a container do not have to be unpacked during the change of transportation. This means it is faster and easier for the cargo to be delivered. This driver is picking up a container of TVs that arrived on a ship from another country.

Often, truck drivers make trips that last several days. On a long haul, two drivers work together. They take turns at the wheel.

A bunk, called a sleeper, is at the back of the cab. One driver sleeps while the other drives. The truck never stops moving except to get fuel or when the truckers stop for food.

Truck drivers like to talk to each other on the road. They speak into special CB radios, as they drive along. They talk about weather conditions, traffic, and delays on their routes.

CB Microphone

Truckers' talk is full of special words. For example, they call a poultry truck a "cackle crate." Here's how one trucker might talk with another:

"Breaker 1-9. This is Big Ed. Come in, please. Over."

"Big Ed, this is Heavy Trucker. Come in. Over."

"Heavy Trucker, I'm in a cackle crate. I had a pumpkin at the piggy bank. Is that your Indian smoke I see at the double-nickle sign over the hill? Can you help? Over."

"Big Ed, I'm in a bobtail. I can help. I'll be right there. 10-4."

Here's what it means:

"May I break in? I'm on channel 1-9. My code name is Big Ed. Please answer."

"My code name is Heavy Trucker. Go ahead."

"I am hauling poultry. I had a flat tire at the tollbooth. Is that your diesel smoke I see at the 55 mile-an-hour sign over the hill? Can you help?"

"I am in a tractor without a semitrailer attached. I can help. I'll be right there. Good-bye."

Truck drivers must know and follow the rules of the road. They plan their routes carefully. A truck may be too heavy for some bridges. It may be too high for some underpasses.

During a trip, a driver keeps a log book. He or she keeps a record of miles traveled and fuel used. Truck repairs are also noted.

Log Book

This driver is carrying a truckload of apples. He has driven six hours today. He has six more hours to go. Off the highway, he sees a truck stop.

With a smile, he pulls up to the truck stop.
It's time for food, fuel, and a good rest.